Spot the Differences

Emu or Ostrich?

by Jamie Rice

Bullfrog
Books

Ideas for Parents and Teachers

Bullfrog Books let children practice reading informational text at the earliest reading levels. Repetition, familiar words, and photo labels support early readers.

Before Reading

• Discuss the cover photo. What does it tell them?

• Look at the picture glossary together. Read and discuss the words.

Read the Book

• "Walk" through the book and look at the photos. Let the child ask questions. Point out the photo labels.

• Read the book to the child, or have him or her read independently.

After Reading

• Prompt the child to think more. Ask: What did you know about emus and ostriches before reading this book? What more would you like to learn?

Bullfrog Books are published by Jump!
5357 Penn Avenue South
Minneapolis, MN 55419
www.jumplibrary.com

Library of Congress Cataloging-in-Publication Data

Names: Rice, Jamie, author.
Title: Emu or ostrich? / by Jamie Rice.
Description: Minneapolis, MN: Jump!, Inc., [2023]
Series: Spot the differences | Includes index.
Audience: Ages 5–8
Identifiers: LCCN 2022011717 (print)
LCCN 2022011718 (ebook)
ISBN 9798885241618 (hardcover)
ISBN 9798885241625 (paperback)
ISBN 9798885241632 (ebook)
Subjects: LCSH: Emus—Juvenile literature.
Ostriches—Juvenile literature.
Classification: LCC QL696.C34 R53 2023 (print)
LCC QL696.C34 (ebook) | DDC 598.5/24—dc23/eng/20220413
LC record available at https://lccn.loc.gov/2022011717
LC ebook record available at https://lccn.loc.gov/2022011718

Editor: Katie Chanez
Designer: Emma Bersie

Photo Credits: Krakenimages.com/Shutterstock, cover (left); a_v_d/Shutterstock, cover (right); Eric Isselee/Shutterstock, 1 (left); Anan Kaewkhammul/Shutterstock, 1 (right); Slowmotiongli/Dreamstime, 3, 10–11, 23br; Cheryl Nelson/Shutterstock, 4; Alen thien/Shutterstock, 5; colacat/Shutterstock, 6–7 (left); Sergei25/Shutterstock, 6–7 (right); MintImages/Shutterstock, 8–9; Schobes/Shutterstock, 12–13; Tuangtong Soraprasert/Shutterstock, 14–15; clearviewstock/Shutterstock, 16–17; David Steele/Shutterstock, 18–19, 23tl, 23bl; pandapaw/Shutterstock, 20 (left); Ken Griffiths/Shutterstock, 20 (right); JaturunThakard/Shutterstock, 21 (left); Sergej Razvodovskij/Shutterstock, 21 (right); Hans Wismeijer/Shutterstock, 22 (left); EcoPrint/Shutterstock, 22 (right); Dirk De Keyser/Dreamstime, 23tr; Vasyl Helevachuk/Dreamstime, 24 (top); NoraphatPhotoss/Shutterstock, 24 (bottom).

Printed in the United States of America at Corporate Graphics in North Mankato, Minnesota.

Table of Contents

How to Use This Book

In this book, you will see pictures of both emus and ostriches. Can you tell which one is in each picture?

Hint: You can find the answers if you flip the book upside down!

Big Birds

This is an emu.

This is an ostrich.

Both are big birds.

They look the same.

But they are not.

How?

Let's see!

Both have feathers.
Emus are dark all over.
Ostriches often have white or pink legs.
Which is this?

Answer: ostrich

feathers

wing

10

Both have dark wings.

An ostrich's have white tips.

Which is this?

An emu has a dark beak.

An ostrich's is light.

Which is this?

beak

toe

Neither bird can fly.

But they run fast!

Toes help.

Ostriches have two.

Emus have three.

Whose feet are these?

Both lay big eggs.

Emu eggs are dark green.

Ostrich eggs are white.

Who laid these?

egg

chick

Chicks hatch!

Emu chicks have stripes.

Ostrich chicks do not.

Which are these?

See and Compare

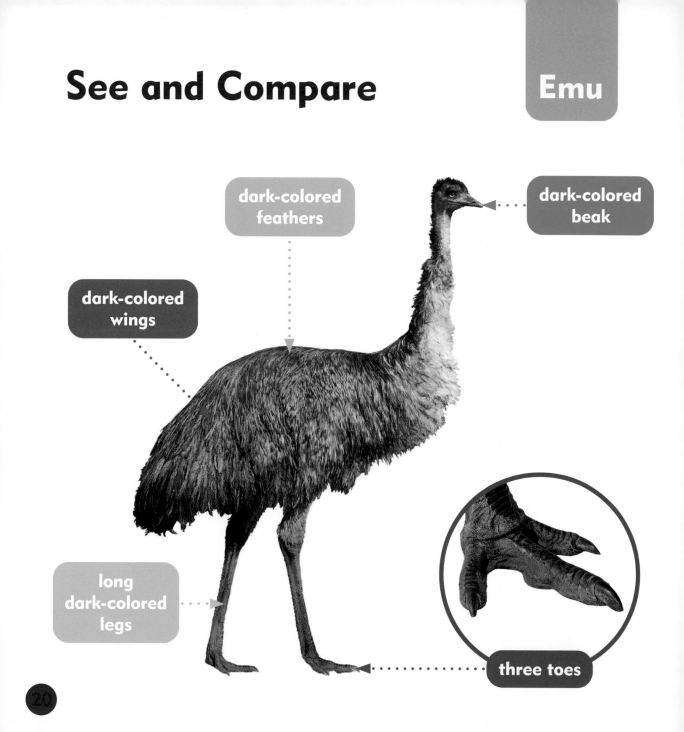

dark-colored feathers

dark-colored beak

dark-colored wings

long dark-colored legs

three toes

20

Ostrich

dark-colored feathers

dark-colored wings with white tips

light-colored beak

long pink or white legs

two toes

21

Quick Facts

Emus and ostriches are big birds. They can't fly, but they run fast. They eat plants and insects and live in hot, dry environments. They are similar, but they have differences. Take a look!

Emus

- often live in wooded areas
- live in Australia
- can be up to seven feet (2.1 meters) tall
- weigh up to 130 pounds (59 kilograms)
- can run 31 miles (50 kilometers) per hour

Ostriches

- often live in the desert
- live in Africa
- can be up to nine feet (2.7 meters) tall
- weigh up to 320 pounds (145 kilograms)
- can run 43 miles (69 kilometers) per hour

Picture Glossary

chicks
Young birds.

hatch
To break out of an egg.

stripes
Thin bands of color.

tips
The end parts or points
of something.

Index

To Learn More

Finding more information is as easy as 1, 2, 3.

❶ Go to www.factsurfer.com

❷ Enter "emuorostrich?" into the search box.

❸ Choose your book to see a list of websites.

SPOT THE DIFFERENCES

Can you spot the differences between bees and wasps? What about alligators and crocodiles? Learn how to tell the differences between similar animals with this fun, interactive series! Have you read them all?

- ALLIGATOR OR CROCODILE?
- BEE OR WASP?
- BUTTERFLY OR MOTH?
- CHEETAH OR LEOPARD?
- CROW OR RAVEN?
- DOLPHIN OR PORPOISE?
- EAGLE OR FALCON?
- EMU OR OSTRICH?
- FROG OR TOAD?
- GRASSHOPPER OR CRICKET?
- HEDGEHOG OR PORCUPINE?
- LIZARD OR SALAMANDER?
- LLAMA OR ALPACA?
- RABBIT OR HARE?
- TURTLE OR TORTOISE?
- WOLF OR COYOTE?

jump!

www.jumplibrary.com
www.jumplibrary.com/teachers

IL: Grades K–3   GRL: E

ISBN 979-8-88524-162-5

90000

9 798885 241625